YELLOWSTONE

for Kids

ISBN-13: 979-8-9893018-0-5

Manufactured in the United States of America

Published in the United States by

Bangtail Press
P.O. Box 11262
Bozeman, MT 59719

www.bangtailpress.com

For Corey

This is Yellowstone National Park

It's a pretty amazing place. It's one of the few places in the world where you might see a grizzly bear from the road. You might even glimpse a wolf or two. But even if you don't see a bear or wolves, you'll likely see bison. In fact, they may be in the middle of the road, creating a traffic jam as you drive through the Park.

You can also stand near Old Faithful and watch it erupt. Or walk down to the Grand Canyon of the Yellowstone and think about how much water it took to carve through all that rock. Or you can walk around on the boardwalks of Mammoth Hot Springs.

The place is so amazing that, on March 1, 1872, America made it our first National Park. The President and Congress thought that no one person should have the right to keep a place like this all to themselves. They thought that it should be for the "benefit and enjoyment of the people."

Those are the very words that are on the entry arch at Mammoth Hot Springs. In a given year, as many as four million people might visit Yellowstone, benefitting from the vision of the early founders.

There's nowhere else like it in the world.

History and Nature

We all know what history is. History is the story of what happened before the present day. To really understand a place, you need to know its history. How did we all come to be where we are?

But the story of Yellowstone Park is not only about the human history. It's also about the natural history. It's the

story of bison recovery and bears and wolf reintroductions. It's the story of first peoples and early expeditions and raging forest fires and ancient volcanoes and hot springs glowing blue. It's the story of everything that had to happen in order for you to see the Park as it exists today.

It's a really good story!

The Volcano

Many of the marvelous features of Yellowstone Park are there because of what's happening underground. It turns out that Yellowstone sits on one of the world's largest volcanoes.

A volcano happens when hot melted rock, or magma, from deep underground rises up through the Earth's crust. Sometimes the magma rises too far or too fast and it erupts out onto the surface. Some of the most famous mountains in the world are actually old volcanoes that have erupted and then cooled.

The Yellowstone volcano has seen at least three big eruptions. The most recent big one was 640,000 years ago. There were some smaller eruptions after that, including one 174,000 years ago that made the West Thumb of Yellowstone Lake.

Another eruption isn't likely to happen anytime soon, but the hot magma that made those eruptions is still there, heating Yellowstone from underneath. It's what has created Old Faithful and Mammoth Hot Springs and Grand Prismatic Spring and a lot of the other famous Yellowstone sites.

The magma under Yellowstone is made up of two big blobs. The smallest one is about 3 to 10 miles beneath the surface. It's around 55 miles long and 25 miles wide. A second blob, 4.5 times bigger, is 12 to 30 miles underground.

The light brown part of this diagram shows the caldera, or mouth, of the last big eruption from 640,000 years ago. That caldera is mostly invisible now.

Yellowstone's First People

The first people appeared in what would become Yellowstone Park after the last ice age. This was around 13,000 years ago. As the ice melted and the Yellowstone region warmed, people began to move in.

At least 27 different Indian tribes came to spend time in the area that would become Yellowstone Park. The Crow called it the "land of the burning ground." The Flatheads called it "smoke from the ground." The Kiowa called it the "place of hot water."

The only modern tribe to live in the area full time was a band of Mountain Shoshone called the Tukudika, or Sheep Eaters. They even lived in the Park for a few years after it was established in 1872.

Yellowstone was known for many things among Native Americans. One of the most important was as the source of a special type of rock used to make arrowheads and tools. This rock was a kind of volcanic glass called obsidian. Blades made with obsidian can be sharper than even a surgeon's scalpel. Obsidian from Yellowstone was so highly prized that it was traded as far east as Ohio.

Frontier photographer William Henry Jackson took this 1870 photo of a band of Mountain Shoshone in Wyoming's Wind River Range, southeast of today's Yellowstone National Park.

Early Explorers

The first Easterners to see what would become Yellowstone were likely mountain men. These were the guys who traveled around the West, trapping beavers to be made into hats.

John Colter was part of the Lewis and Clark Expedition sent by President Thomas Jefferson to explore the Northwest. As Lewis and Clark returned from their trip, Colter went off on his own. In 1807, he likely saw Yellowstone Lake, but he left no written account.

In 1827, trapper Daniel Potts wrote to his brother in Pennsylvania, describing what was probably the West Thumb Geyser Basin. His letters are the first written descriptions of the area. "On the south borders of this lake is a number of hot and boiling springs—some of water and others of most beautiful fine clay." Other early mountain men who visited the region included Joe Meek and Osborne Russell.

By the middle of the 1840s, the mountain man era was over, but the rumors of Yellowstone had been seeded and were starting to grow. The world was becoming curious. What was this amazing place in the mountains of the American West?

Alfred Jacob Miller

Alfred Jacob Miller was one of the first accomplished artists to travel west of the Mississippi. In 1837, he saw the waning days of the mountain men. His paintings are some of the only firsthand depictions we have of this famous part of American history.

"The first Spring we visited was about 10 feet in diameter which threw up mud with a noise similar to boiling soap . . . along the side of a small ridge the hot steam rushed forth from holes in the ground."

Osborne Russell
1838

First Expeditions

As people began hearing stories about Yellowstone, there was a lot of curiosity but some disbelief, too. Could all those geysers and waterfalls and canyons in the stories actually be real? Three early expeditions played a big part in showing the world that the tales were true.

In 1869, the Folsom-Cook-Peterson Expedition braved "Indian trouble" to visit Tower Fall, the Grand Canyon of the Yellowstone, Mud Volcano, Yellowstone Lake, and the Firehole geyser basins. A year later, the Washburn-Langford-Doane Expedition saw Tower Fall, Canyon, and Yellowstone Lake. They also named Old Faithful. In 1871, the Hayden Geological Survey included scientists, mapmakers, a photographer, and two artists. The Hayden Survey showed the world just how incredible Yellowstone was.

These expeditions helped encourage Congress and President Ulysses S. Grant to create Yellowstone National Park on March 1, 1872.

The Hayden Survey included an early odometer. A cart pulled behind a mule could count the number of times its wheels went around, giving the Survey's mapmakers a good idea of how far they had traveled.

Geologist Ferdinand Hayden led an 1871 survey to Yellowstone. This photograph by William Henry Jackson shows the Survey's pack train, including their odometer. These were the first wheels to roll through what would become Yellowstone.

Folsom-Cook-Peterson

David Folsom, upper left, Charles Cook, upper right, and William Peterson were all part of the first organized expedition to the Yellowstone region.

Washburn-Langford-Doane

Henry Washburn, upper left, Nathaniel Langford, upper right, and Lieutenant Gustavus Doane were part of the group that named Old Faithful.

Flight of the Nez Perce

In 1877, just five years after the creation of Yellowstone Park, a band of Nez Perce Indians fled through the new Park, chased by the US Army. In violation of an earlier treaty, the Army wanted to force them to live on a reservation. The Indians didn't want to go.

In June of 1877, a group of about 750 Nez Perce men, women, and children in Eastern Oregon started an epic journey. On August 23, and after several battles with the Army, they entered Yellowstone Park. They went in close to where West Yellowstone is today. Thirteen days later, they exited to the east.

During their time in Yellowstone, they encountered about 25 visitors. They took a few of these early tourists hostage, and tragically killed two of them.

The Nez Perce went on to surrender in October, in Montana's Bears Paw Mountains

A kiosk on Grand Loop Road commemorates a spot near where, on August 23, 1877, more than 600 Nez Perce camped along with their 2,000 horses. The kiosk is very close to Nez Perce Creek.

just south of Canada. After their flight was over, Chief Joseph of the Nez Perce gave a very famous speech. In that speech, he said, “From where the sun now stands, I will fight no more forever.”

White Bird

Yellow Wolf

Chief Joseph

Looking Glass

Ollokot

Chief Joseph and other tribal leaders fought several battles with the US Army over the course of 1,170 miles. Generals Oliver Howard and Nelson Miles and Colonels John Gibbon and Samuel Sturgis were among those officers involved in the pursuit.

John Gibbon

Samuel Sturgis

Oliver Otis Howard

Nelson Miles

The Army in Yellowstone

The US Congress created Yellowstone even before there was a National Park Service to run it. In the Park's early years, there were rules against hunting animals and taking souvenirs away from the geysers and hot springs, but there wasn't really anyone around to enforce them. So they called in the cavalry.

In 1886, Captain Moses Harris and Company M, First Cavalry arrived in Mammoth Hot Springs. There were only about 60 men at first but they were tasked with protecting the whole Park.

Five years later, in 1891, the first buildings of what came to be Fort Yellowstone in Mammoth Hot Springs were completed. By 1910, there were 324 soldiers stationed in Mammoth. These troops had their work cut out for them. Only about 500 people visited the Park in 1880 but by 1910 that number had grown to 19,000.

By 1918, the Park was fully under National Park Service control, and the Army was reassigned. Many of Fort Yellowstone's original buildings can still be seen in Mammoth.

At its largest, Fort Yellowstone housed as many as 324 enlisted soldiers and their families. This F. Jay Haynes photo shows the fort in 1895.

Philetus Norris, left, was the second superintendent of Yellowstone (after Nathaniel Langford), and the first to be paid for the position. He served from 1877 to 1882.

Harry Yount was Yellowstone's first "gamekeeper," or early Park ranger. His efforts to protect wildlife and his recognition of the role of enforcement made him an important figure in the history of the Park Service.

Old Faithful

Geysers happen when underground water, confined in a certain way, gets hot enough to boil over and spew up like a fountain. Yellowstone is home to more than 500 geysers. That's over half of all the geysers in the world!

The most famous of these is Old Faithful. It was named for how predictably it erupts. It's not perfect, though. The time between eruptions in the 1870s was around 60 to 70 minutes. Now it erupts about every 94 minutes, give or take 10 minutes.

Most Old Faithful eruptions will spew water somewhere between 100 and 180 feet up in the air. To give you an idea of how tall this is, if you took five school buses and set them end to end, they would still only be about 175 feet tall.

People travel from all over to see Old Faithful. They know that once they're standing on those famous boardwalks, within a few minutes they'll get to see one of the most incredible sights in the world.

"It spouted at regular intervals nine times during our stay, the columns of boiling water being thrown from ninety to one hundred and twenty-five feet at each discharge . . . We gave it the name of 'Old Faithful.'"

Nathanial Langford
1870

Old Faithful Underground

What you see happening above ground in Old Faithful is only part of the story. There's a whole lot going on under the ground as well.

Geysers occur because there's a kind of plumbing system in the ground beneath them. Groundwater, heated up by magma (rock so hot that it has melted) turns to steam. If the conditions are right— if there is a crack that leads to the surface and if that crack is especially tight—then the pressure of the steam builds and builds until it finally pushes water to the surface all at once, causing an eruption.

Old Faithful's water comes from a source about 100 yards away from its vent. Part of this reservoir of groundwater is under the historic Old Faithful Inn. After Old Faithful erupts, new groundwater starts seeping in, boiling and turning to steam and starting the whole process over again.

A groundwater reservoir that feeds into Old Faithful holds almost 80 million gallons of water. It's not really a pool of water, though. It's more like a network of cracks filled with flowing water. Each eruption of Old Faithful takes about 8,000 gallons from this reservoir. It's replenished by snowmelt and rain and the nearby Firehole River.

Hot Springs

There are more than 10,000 hydrothermal features in Yellowstone. Hydro means water and thermal means hot. These sites include geysers, fumaroles (steam vents), and most of all, hot springs.

The largest hot spring in the Park is the Grand Prismatic Spring. It's 200 feet across, making it the third largest in the world. At its hottest, it's 189 degrees Farhenheit. That's about the same temperature as the very hottest cup of coffee.

Hot water bubbles up from under Grand Prismatic and spills over into the nearby Firehole River. Minerals dissolve in the water and build up on the banks, giving the spring a layered look around its edges. In the water itself, different kinds of bacteria live in different heat zones, giving it different colors. The water in the middle is too hot for anything to live there, though. That's why it's such a perfect blue.

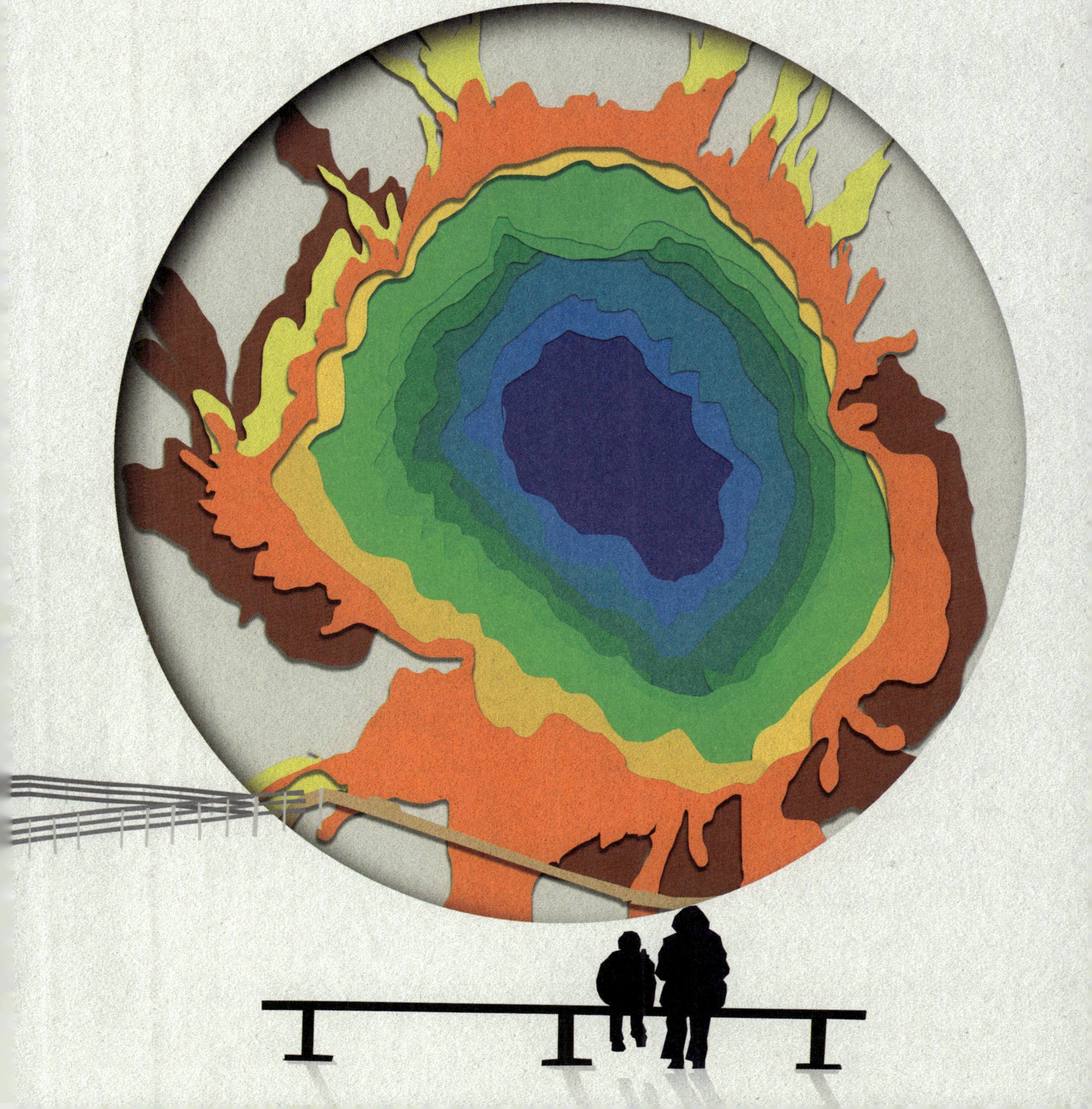

Grand Canyon of the Yellowstone

There are about 290 waterfalls in Yellowstone Park. The most impressive of these are probably the Upper and Lower Falls in the Grand Canyon of the Yellowstone.

The Lower Falls is 308 feet tall. That is taller than two Statues of Liberty! The Upper Falls is 109 feet tall. The canyon is about 17 miles long and between 820 and 1,150 feet deep.

It's a little surprising that the canyon isn't really, in the big picture, all that old. Geologists think that between 10,000 and 18,000 years ago, ice dams may have repeatedly blocked the Yellowstone River. As the dams broke and the river rushed out, the floods scraped out the canyon, over and over again.

In 1869, Charles Cook, of the Folsom-Cook Expedition, described his first sight of the canyon: "I sat there in amazement, while my companions came up," he wrote, "and after that, it seemed to me that it was five minutes before anyone spoke."

ARTIST POINT
MAIN ROAD

Mammoth Hot Springs

On the northern end of the Park, Mammoth Hot Springs is often the first thing that visitors from Montana get to see.

And there's *a lot* to see! There are flat pools with terraces and there are big mounds that look like ice cream with water trickling over them and there are vents that just steam. Most of it is made of a special kind of rock called travertine.

Unlike other hot springs in the Park, Mammoth has limestone in the ground underneath it. As the hot water seeps to the surface, it dissolves the limestone and creates something called *calcium carbonate*. This is the same stuff you also find in snail shells and pearls. As the water runs over the surface, it deposits calcium carbonate, gradually building it up into travertine.

When you visit Mammoth, you'll see boardwalks all around the hot springs. These boardwalks go on for about 1.75 miles! You can get in a pretty good hike just by going up and down the boardwalks. The hot springs are very fragile, and dangerously hot. Never *ever* step off the boardwalks!

Mud Pots

What are some of your favorite smells in the world? Maybe the lawn right after it's been cut? Or baking bread? Or hamburgers on the grill?

If you're one of the scientists who studies the mud pots in Yellowstone, your favorite smell might just be rotten eggs.

The most famous mud pots in Yellowstone—Artist Paint Pots south of Norris Geyser Basin, Mud Volcano north of Yellowstone Lake, and Fountain Paint Pots in the Lower Geyser Basin north of Old Faithful—smell a little bit like rotten eggs. That's the smell of a gas called *hydrogen sulfide*.

Mud pots are hot springs that don't have as much water. They're formed when water on the surface dissolves rock into muddy clay, and then gas or water vapor heated from underneath pushes up through the mud, making bubbles. When some of the rocks are dissolved, hydrogen sulfide is released.

It's an odd and wonderful sight, seeing all that mud, which should be solid and firm, bubble and roil in slow motion.

Geologist Ferdinand Hayden, during his 1871 expedition to Yellowstone, said that the Mud Volcano was "the greatest marvel we have met with."

Fountain
Paint Pots

Yellowstone Lake

If Yellowstone Park was a door, its hinge would be Yellowstone Lake. If the Park was a wheel, the axle would be the lake. If it was an airplane, its propeller would be . . . well, you get the idea.

Yellowstone Lake is the largest, high-altitude lake in North America, and in some ways it's kind of the heart of Yellowstone Park. The surface is at an elevation of more than 7,700 feet, which means the water is always very cold, even in August. If you went swimming in Yellowstone Lake without a wetsuit, you might only be able to survive for 20 or 30 minutes. And it completely freezes over in the

The first named boat in Yellowstone Lake was the "Annie," launched by members of the 1871 Hayden Geological Survey. William Henry Jackson took this photo.

LC-USZ62-52479

winter. Some of the winter ice is almost three feet thick.

There's also a lot going on under the surface. Scientists recently looked at the lake bottom and saw that it has many of the same features you see elsewhere in Yellowstone, including geysers, canyons, rock spires, and vents. Hydrothermal activity is especially apparent on the West Thumb side. There are trails and boardwalks that will take you around some very interesting cones and hot springs.

When you look out over that calm lake, just keep in mind that it's covering another, hidden version of Yellowstone Park.

Hiking and Fishing in Yellowstone

There are 251 miles of roads in Yellowstone Park, but there are more than 900 miles of hiking trails. If you really want to know what Yellowstone is like, it might help to take a walk off the road.

It's hard to say just how many people go hiking in Yellowstone in a year, but it's not all that many. If you do get away from the paved roads and parking lots, you'll be one of Yellowstone's elite visitors!

When they go hiking, a lot of people will bring a fishing rod with them. The fishing can be very good. There's a kind of trout called Yellowstone cutthroat which is hard to find outside the Park. They're beautiful and really fun to catch, too.

If you and your parents decide to go hiking or fishing, make sure you read all the rules first. Fishing in Yellowstone is different than fishing in nearby Montana, Wyoming, or Idaho. You should also bring maps, snacks, water, and bear spray. You never know when you might surprise a grizzly on the trail.

Artists in Yellowstone

Painters and photographers have been inspired by Yellowstone Park since even before it was a park. The most famous of these artists was probably Thomas Moran. His paintings of Yellowstone from the Hayden Survey in 1871 helped make Yellowstone a National Park. His journal and sketchbook are on display at the Albright Visitor Center in Mammoth.

Photographer William Henry Jackson was also on the Hayden Survey. His photos show us a little bit of what life was like for travelers in 1871.

Photographer F. Jay Haynes was a photographer who had a studio in Mammoth in the late 1800s and early 1900s. He sold millions of post-cards. His first visit to Yellowstone was in 1881, just ten years after Jackson and Moran.

F. Jay Haynes had a studio in Mammoth. His photos and postcards, including this 1887 image of "Castle Geyser and Skiers" helped show the world what a magical place Yellowstone was.

Artist Thomas Moran was part of the Hayden Geological Survey in 1871. His paintings complemented Jackson's photos. Together, their images helped convince America that Yellowstone was worth preserving. His huge painting, "Grand Canyon of the Yellowstone," was created in 1872 and for a while hung in the halls of Congress.

The first person to photograph what became Yellowstone National Park was William Henry Jackson. He was part of the Hayden Geological Survey in 1871. His images, like this photo of Mammoth Hot Springs, are now important historical documents.

Bison

When people think of Yellowstone, they often think of bison, also called buffalo. Most visitors to the Park will see at least a few. The Hayden and Lamar Valleys are especially good places to see them.

Bison are big! Some of them can weigh up to 2,200 pounds. And while they may look slow, they're actually really fast. Every year, a few tourists are hurt or even killed by bison. Don't get too close!

The real story about the bison in Yellowstone, though, is how they almost disappeared. Two hundred years ago, there were as many as 60 million bison in North America. For Indians on the Great Plains, bison were a huge part of their lives, providing food, shelter, and utensils.

After the Civil War, bison were almost entirely shot out by market hunters and the US Army. By 1902, there was a small herd of only 23 bison remaining in Yellowstone. This was the largest wild herd of bison south of Canada.

Today there are more than 5,000 bison in the Park. Bison recovery in Yellowstone is one of the great conservation success stories of our time.

Wolves

Yellowstone is home to 67 different species of mammals, including rare species like lynx and wolverines and grizzly bears. For a long time, wolves were not included in that list.

Wolves are predators, which means that they need to kill and eat other animals in order to live. This has sometimes made them unpopular. They were legally hunted and poisoned in Yellowstone even after the Park was established. This was before we knew what an important role predators can play in an ecosystem. By the 1970s, there were probably no wolves in Yellowstone.

But then in 1995 and 1996, wolves were reintroduced to the Park. Thirty-one wolves were captured in Canada, brought to Yellowstone, and released.

Yellowstone now has all the species of mammals it had before Europeans arrived!

Wolves, left, are much larger than coyotes, bottom right. Wolves also have blockier snouts, rounded ears, and shorter tails.

Today there are at least 108 wolves in Yellowstone in 10 different packs. There are many more outside the Park. In 2021, Montana estimated that there were 1,160 wolves in the state.

Wolf watching is a big part of tourism in Yellowstone. When you see clusters of people on the side of the road with spotting scopes and cameras on tripods, they may be watching wolves.

Grizzly Bears

Few wilderness experiences are as exciting as seeing a grizzly bear. There aren't that many wild places in the world where you can still glimpse one of these large, fierce, beautiful bears. Yellowstone is one of them!

In all of Yellowstone Park, though, there are only 150 to 200 grizzly bears. If you do get to see one, you will be very lucky indeed.

Yellowstone also has black bears, which are smaller and not as aggressive as grizzlies. There are more black bears than grizzly bears in Yellowstone. If you see a bear, even if it's brownish or reddish, chances are pretty good it will be a black bear rather than a grizzly. It's important to know how to tell them apart. Grizzlies have shoulder humps, rounded ears, and longer claws. When they're standing on all fours, their hips are lower than their shoulders.

Grizzly bears, left, have a conspicuous shoulder hump. At a distance, the hump may be the easiest way to tell them apart from black bears, bottom right.

All the Wildlife

Wolves, grizzly bears, and bison receive most of the attention in Yellowstone, but there is a lot more going on with the wildlife than just these three species. There are bighorn sheep and mountain goats and mule deer and mountain lions and . . .

Rocky Mountain elk are one of the more plentiful species in the Park, although they are sometimes hard to spot. If you are in the Park in the fall and if you're very lucky, you might get to hear a bull elk bugle. It's one of the most beautiful sounds in the world.

Moose are also in the Park, although they are not as plentiful as they used to be. The population is in decline throughout the West. If you are lucky enough to see a moose, it's almost as special as seeing a grizzly bear!

As for birds, there are as many as 285 different species that can be found in the Park at one time or another. And there are at least 150 different species that nest in the Park!

Always remember that the wildlife in Yellowstone can be dangerous. Don't get too close!

affected the Park. Nine of those fires were caused by people.

Before the fire season was over, almost 800,000 acres of Yellowstone had burned. That was around 36 percent of the whole Park!

Seeing so much of Yellowstone burn was very difficult for a lot of people, but there were important lessons to the fires as well. Forest fires are an essential part of the wilderness ecology. In order for there to be new growth, the old growth sometimes has to burn away. That's what happened in Yellowstone.

As you drive through the Park today, you'll see that some patches of pine trees are smaller than some of the other trees just down the road. That may be the new growth that started right after 1988.

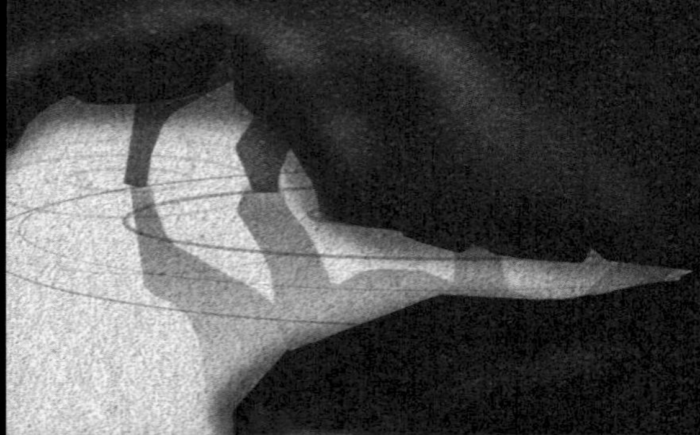

Acknowledgments

Books of this sort rely on the work of writers and artists who came before. It's important to acknowledge their contribution.

The drawings of the magma blob on page 9 and of the plumbing under Old Faithful on page 23 are my drawings but they're based on the work of several other people. Also, keep in mind that these drawings aren't really all that precise. They're just meant to give you an idea. When you visit Old Faithful, be sure and see the Visitor Education Center. They have a lot more information than I can share with you here.

I relied on several different books to write this, but *Yellowstone National Park: The First 150 Years* by Jeff Henry and *Searching for Yellowstone: Ecology and Wonder in the Last Wilderness* by Paul Schullery were especially helpful.

I'm also grateful to my mom and dad who showed me Yellowstone for the first time when I was about nine years old. That was almost 45 years ago now. Thank you to all the parents who are wise enough to show their kids this amazing place!